Kyle L. Miller
Illustrations by Randon T. Eddy

Jungle House Publications

Many thanks go to family, friends and colleagues whose expertise, help and support made this book a joy to write and produce. My gratitude goes to: Dr. Sidney B. Simon, always my mentor and supporter, Linda Salisbury, of Tabby House, who helped guide me through the art of condensation and consistency, Randon Eddy, for her incredible artistic talent, Pat Kiely, Priscilla Friedersdorf, Claudia Burns, Carol and Bill Burns, Melanie and Jan Wiford, Carol Rothman, Sylvia Drew, Sue Acker, and Alice and Nick Masci. A special thanks to Bev Postmus, a well-respected authority on birds, who helped with the accuracy of the bird descriptions. And thanks to Susie Holly, of WindWord Editorial Services.

Cover and book design: Maggie Rogers, MaggieMay Designs
Illustrations by Randon T. Eddy

Summary: During a snowy plover's quest to hatch her eggs, twelve shorebirds and a ghost crab team up to help protect her eggs from predators for twenty-four days.

Juvenile fiction, Grades 2-5

ISBN: 10 0-9769332-3-3
ISBN: 13 978-0-9769332-3-6
Library of Congress Control Number: 2010909701

Manufactured by Friesens Corporation in Altona, MB Canada
September 2010 #57792

Also by Kyle L. Miller: *DILLO–A Baby Armadillo's Adventure on Sanibel Island*

The new contact information is:
Kyle L. Miller
15998 Mandolin Bay Dr. # 102
Fort Myers, FL 33908
239-689-8843
Kmiller765@aol.com

CONTENTS

This book is dedicated to snowy plovers

and endangered animal species all over the world,
and to those who support and protect them.

INTRODUCTION

Snowy Pea and the Ghost Crab is a story about a tiny snowy plover shorebird whose greatest wish in life is to hatch her eggs. Many of the birds on the beach befriend Snowy Pea and make a plan to help her realize her dream. The story is obviously fictional. The animals are real, but in the story they are anthropomorphic (pronounced: an-thro-po-mor-fik), which means they act in human ways, not in ways that are typical for their species. For instance, ghost crabs are the most prevalent predators of snowy plover eggs and chicks. Fish crows, ring-bill gulls, laughing gulls, and ruddy turnstones are also known to eat other birds' eggs. But even though some of the behaviors of the birds are not real, the descriptions of the dangers to the snowy plover eggs and chicks are. The beautiful little snowy plover has become endangered on the Pacific Coast and threatened on the Gulf Coast because of loss of habitat due to predators, human interaction, and weather.

This story was written not only to entertain and educate, but also to bring awareness to the reader of how difficult the survival of many species has become in our world. Enjoy learning about these birds and creatures common to many coastal beaches. Hopefully, after reading, *Snowy Pea and the Ghost Crab*, time spent at the seashore will take on a whole new fun way of looking at wildlife, while appreciating and protecting their existence.

For your convenience, a description of the characters in this book has been placed before the story so you may become familiar with the names and images of the wildlife.

Cast of Characters

To help you identify the birds in the story, the following animal characters are listed with the character name first and the real name second. The size of the birds are average, and the interesting facts are brief. For more information about each of the animals, see the list of references at the end of this section. You can listen to sounds and watch videos on the internet.

***Snowy Pea*—Snowy Plover**: 6 inches. First flight is approximately 30 days after hatching. Their large eyes help them to see prey on sandy beaches. They eat by pausing, running, and pecking at the ground for insects, small shells, and marine worms. They are the same color as the sand and very hard to see on the beach. Their nests are often surrounded by stakes and string on beaches to protect them from beach-walkers. They are considered threatened in Florida.

***Ghosty Ghost Crab*—Ghost Crab**: 2-4 inches. Besides eating baby sea turtles, and bird chicks, they like sand fleas, coquinas, mole crabs, lizards, and carrion. They can run sideways, forward, and backward at speeds up to 10 miles per hour. Its large eyestalks are capable of 360° vision. In the winter ghost crabs hibernate in their burrows, "holding their breath" for six weeks by storing oxygen in specialized sacs near their gills.

***Oscar Osprey*—Osprey**: 22 inches. They mainly eat fish. They hover over the water and plunge feet first when they spot prey. Osprey carry fish headfirst as aerodynamically as possible. They often build nests on manmade structures, such as telephone poles, channel markers, duck blinds, and nest platforms designed especially for them. They reuse nests year after year. They are one of the most widespread birds in the world, found on all continents except Antarctica.

***Paulie Pelican*—Brown Pelican**: 45 inches. They are noted for their spectacular head-first dives to trap unsuspecting fish in their expandable pouches. A preen (oil) gland is located near the base of the tail. They use their long bill and the back of their head to spread the oil to all their feathers. This keeps pelicans from becoming waterlogged as they swim and dive. They weighs 6-12 pounds and has a wingspan from 6 to 8 feet.

***Edna Egret*—Great Egret**: 39 inches. They are large white herons with yellow bills and black legs. They feed on fish, amphibians, insects, reptiles, and small mammals. The Great Egret is the logo for one of the oldest conservation and environmental organizations in the United States, the National Audubon Society.

***Crazy Crow*—Fish Crow**: 17 inches. Fish crows are smaller than the American crows and are often seen around beaches, dumpsters, and parking lots. They are very intelligent and very good at rummaging through picnic baskets and bags left unattended on the beach. They eat amphibians, crabs, fish, shrimps, bird eggs, and picnic leftovers.

***Willie Willet*—Willet**: 15 inches. Willets are known by their piercing calls and bright black-and-white flashing wings. A large sandpiper, they eat insects, crustaceans, mollusks, grasses, and seeds. They are often seen on beaches probing the sand with their long, heavy bill.

***Iris Ibis*—White Ibis**: 25 inches. Ibis eat crayfish, mud crabs, aquatic insects, and frogs. In Florida, their habitat is threatened by development, pollution, and water management. There are also Scarlet (red) Ibis and Glossy (black) Ibis that can also be seen in Florida.

***Joker Laughing Gull*—Laughing Gull**: 17 inches. They have a light, buoyant flight and a high-pitched laugh, "ha, ha, ha, ha." Unlike many larger gulls, Laughing Gulls seldom steal the eggs or chicks of other birds. They feed on fish, crustaceans, worms, carrion, garbage, and picnic food.

Ringer Ring-bill—**Ring-billed Gull**: 19 inches. These gulls frequent parking lots and southern coastal beaches in the winter. They eat garbage, insects, earthworms, fish, rodents, and other seabird eggs. They can be found along coastal waterways, but many of these gulls never see anything except freshwater all their lives.

Ruddy Turnstone—**Ruddy Turnstone**: 8 inches. With their strong, wedge-shaped bill, they feed by turning over stones, shells, seaweed, and other objects. They eat invertebrates, small fish, carrion, human garbage, and unattended eggs of other bird species. They also eat scraps from picnics.

Sandy Sanderling—**Sanderling**: 7 inches. These birds are small sandpipers and often mistaken for plovers. Always in motion, they frequently chase waves back and forth looking for tiny coquinas. They eat small crabs, worms, mollusks, and insects. In the winter they are one of the whitest shorebirds on the beach.

Blacky Belly—**Black-bellied Plover**: 11 inches. They feed on marine worms, crustaceans, and mollusks on the shore. They are the largest of the plovers and weigh six times more than a Snowy Plover. They are often called the sentinels of the beach as they give a clear, loud whistle when they perceive danger.

Royal Tern—**Royal Tern**: 20 inches. Royal Terns have a distinctive crest of black feathers and a long orange bill. They dive into the water from 40 to 50 feet high to catch fish. Sometimes they steal fish, especially from the Brown Pelican. Nesting colonies can reach 10,000 along the Gulf Coast.

Ringtail Raccoon—**Raccoon**: 10 pounds. Their diet includes fruits, nuts, seeds, vegetables, roots, amphibians, reptiles, fish, birds, bird and turtle eggs, insects, and garbage. While feeding in the water, raccoons frequently wet their hand-like paws to enhance their sense of touch. They have the ability to open coolers and other camping equipment.

***Harry Herring Gull*—Herring Gull**: 25 inches. They eat garbage, clams, fish, rodents, insects, eggs and chicks of other birds. A common gull, they often drop clams and other shellfish on exposed rocks or parking lots in order to break the shells and get to the soft interior.

***Sneaky Slicker Snake*—Black Racer**: 3-6 feet. These snakes are black with white on the chin and throat. The iris of their eyes are usually red or orange. They are non-poisonous and eat frogs, lizards, birds and their eggs, snakes, and rodents. They live mostly inland, but may occasionally look for prey on the beach.

***Dandy Dog*—Dog**: The dog in the story is a labrador mix. But in general, any dog, big or small, when not on a leash, loves to run on the sand and might step on bird eggs. They also chase birds for fun. This tires the birds which are on the beach to eat and rest.

Glossary:

1. **Coquina**: tiny shells that dig into the sand when the waves recede.
2. **Crustacean:** an animal that has a hard shell, like a crab, shrimp, or lobster.
3. **Invertebrate**: an animal that does not have a backbone, e.g. an insect or worm.
4. **Mollusk**: an invertebrate with a soft unsegmented body, usually protected by a shell.
5. **Mole crab:** a small crustacean that lives in the sand of tidal beaches. Sometimes called a "sand flea" and a "sand crab," they are also used for bait.
6. **Sand Flea**: a tiny black gnat, also called a "no-see-um." They come out early morning and early evening as biting pests that leave little red spots on the skin.

References:

The Cornell Lab of Ornithology, www.allaboutbirds.org.
America's Wildlife Resource, www.eNature.com
Field Guide to Birds, Stokes, Donald & Lillian, Little Brown and Co. New York, 1996
Birds of North America, Online, www.bna.birds.cornell.edu/bna

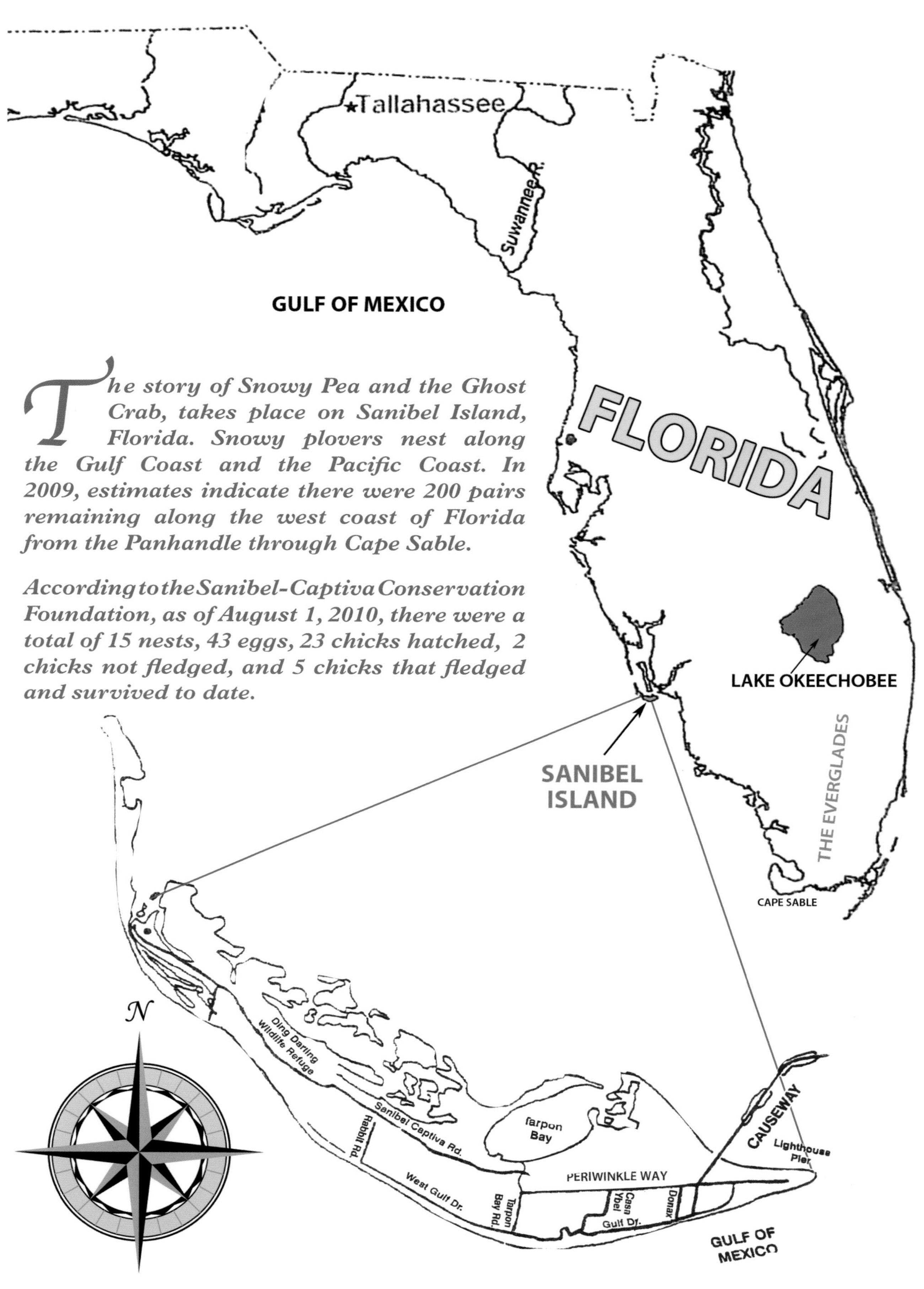

The story of Snowy Pea and the Ghost Crab, takes place on Sanibel Island, Florida. Snowy plovers nest along the Gulf Coast and the Pacific Coast. In 2009, estimates indicate there were 200 pairs remaining along the west coast of Florida from the Panhandle through Cape Sable.

According to the Sanibel-Captiva Conservation Foundation, as of August 1, 2010, there were a total of 15 nests, 43 eggs, 23 chicks hatched, 2 chicks not fledged, and 5 chicks that fledged and survived to date.

ONE
THE RESCUE

Early one April morning Oscar Osprey was flying high above the blue-green waters off the coast of southwest Florida. His eyes were like telescopes as he searched the gently rolling waves for his next fish meal. Most birds of prey have keen eyesight so they can see food from far away. Oscar spotted a school of minnows darting about in the shallow water not far from the shore. There was a delicious-looking sea trout just behind them. Keeping his eyes focused on the fish, Oscar was just about to dive for his breakfast when he was distracted by a cry of distress coming from the beach.

Peep! Peep! Peep! Peep! Peep! Peep!

Oscar looked over toward the beach. He saw a tiny sand-colored bird running around in circles and zigzags. It was dragging one of its wings in the sand as it cried, *Peep! Peep! Peep!* He thought it was hurt. Some birds of prey, such as red-shouldered hawks, would soar down and grab the little bird for breakfast. Ospreys, however, don't eat other birds, only fish.

Peep! Peep! Peep! cried the tiny bird.

Oscar wondered what was wrong. He decided to put off breakfast for a while and flew toward the shore to get a better look. Then he noticed his friend, Paulie Pelican, perched in a tree behind the sand dunes. He flew to the tree and landed on a dead branch just below Paulie. The pelican was also watching the frightened little bird.

"Hi, Paulie," said Oscar. "What's wrong with that bird? Did it break its wing?"

Paulie replied in a low sleepy voice, "She's not hurt. She's just scared. That's Snowy Pea. She's trying to get the attention of Ringtail Raccoon over there by the coconut palm trees. She has a nest of eggs on the sand and doesn't want Ringtail to find them. Snowy plovers pretend they are injured to distract predators away from their nests and babies."

"Predators?" asked Oscar.

"Yeah, you know, living creatures that want to eat you, like sharks and alligators. You are a predator to the fish you eat," said Paulie.

"Hmm," said Oscar, looking at the raccoon. It was sniffing the sand and moving toward Snowy Pea's eggs.

As they watched, Edna, a great egret, joined them on the branch next to Paulie. "What's going on?" she asked. Oscar told Edna about Snowy Pea and Ringtail Raccoon.

"Oh, that poor little thing," Edna said. "I talked to her the other day. She told me that she has tried to hatch her eggs many times on other beaches, but something always destroys them. Once a big dog, who was chasing gulls, stepped on them. Another time a raccoon gobbled them up right in front of her. No wonder she's terrified. She thought this beach would be safer for her eggs. It looks like no beach is safe for snowy plovers."

"That's awful," said Oscar.

Peep! Peep! Peep! cried Snowy Pea, still dragging her wing. Ringtail ignored Snowy Pea and moved closer and closer to her nest.

With a flutter of wings, Crazy Crow, a fish crow, landed on a branch above Edna and Paulie. He was always getting into trouble stealing things from picnic baskets and bags on the beach. One day a human yelled at him, "Get out of there, you crazy crow!" The name stuck.

"I bet you're talking about Snowy Pea," Crazy Crow said in a squawky voice. "I met her yesterday. I saw her eggs and was tempted to grab one when she wasn't looking."

"Crazy Crow! That's terrible!" scolded Edna Egret.

"I know, but I was hungry and eggs are delicious. She begged me not to eat them. She said if I was that hungry, she would help me get food. So she flew over to some humans having a picnic on the beach. She peeped and peeped and dragged her wing right in front of them, just like she's doing now. As they watched her, I flew in behind their chairs and grabbed a bag of potato chips. Boy, they were tasty! It was then I decided Snowy Pea would be my friend forever."

"Wow, that's quite a story, Crazy Crow!" said Oscar. "I guess you're a predator for potato chips," he added, happy that he could use a new word.

They all looked down at the terrified bird. *Peep! Peep! Peep!* Ringtail Raccoon was heading straight toward Snowy Pea's eggs.

"Can't we do something?" asked Edna Egret.

"I know," said Paulie. "Crazy Crow, you fly down and kick sand in that raccoon's face. Oscar, you swoop down and pinch his hind end with your sharp talons."

"OK, I'll do it," said Oscar.

"That's a great idea, Paulie!" said Crazy Crow, all excited. "But why can't I pinch his hind end?"

"Just go, before it's too late!" said Paulie. They both flew out of the tree and dove toward the raccoon.

Before Ringtail knew what was happening, sand was spraying into his eyes. Then he felt an awful pain just above his tail. "Owww!" he cried out, trying to rub the sand out of his eyes. He felt another painful pinch. "Owwweeeee!" he yelled again. He was so scared he turned around and ran away to safety under the bushes at the edge of the beach.

"Yea! Hurrah! Yea!" shouted Edna and Paulie from the tree. Crazy Crow and Oscar flew back up to the branch.

"That was fun!" said Crazy Crow.

"Did you see that raccoon run for his life?" asked Oscar excitedly.

"Good job," said Paulie, happy that his plan worked.

"Way to go, you two," said Edna. "I bet Snowy Pea is happy it's over."

They all looked down and saw Snowy Pea returning to her nest. She nestled down on top of her eggs and almost became invisible since she was the same color as the sand and shells around her.

"I'm going to see if she's all right," said Edna. She pushed off the branch and extended her long white wings.

"I'm going with Edna," said Crazy Crow.

"Let's go, Paulie," said Oscar. "I want to meet her." They flew out of the tree and down to Snowy Pea sitting on her nest.

TWO
Meeting Snowy Pea

Snowy Pea had settled down on top of her eggs trying to recover from her terrifying ordeal with Ringtail Raccoon. She knew it was Crazy Crow who helped scare the raccoon away, but she didn't recognize the other big bird that had helped. She was startled when Edna Egret landed on the sand next to her.

"Oh, Edna, you scared me," Snowy Pea said in her little voice.

"I'm sorry, I just wanted to see if you were OK," said Edna.

Crazy Crow, Paulie Pelican, and Oscar Osprey joined Edna in a semicircle around Snowy Pea.

"Thanks for scaring that raccoon away," Snowy Pea said. "I've never seen a bird attack a raccoon before." They all laughed.

"I'm happy to help," Oscar said, feeling proud of himself.

"I saw you yesterday," Snowy Pea said to Oscar. "You just dropped down from the sky and grabbed a big fish out of the water with your feet. That fish looked heavy."

"Yeah, it was big," replied Oscar. "I thought it was going to drag me back down to the water."

"Why didn't you let go of it?" asked Snowy Pea.

"Once my talons grab onto a fish, it's hard to let go," explained Oscar. He held up one of his feet. It had three long toes with razor-sharp curved talons and one thumb opposite the toes. "See? These are my talons. I can even turn this toe around and use it as an extra thumb so those slimy fish can't wiggle free."

"I'm so lucky you were here this morning, Oscar. You helped save my eggs," Snowy Pea said. "Do you live near here?"

"My nest is across the river at the top of a Norfolk pine tree. My mate, Olive, and I have nested there for years," said Oscar.

"I bet you don't have any problems hatching your chicks in the top of a tree," said Snowy Pea.

"One time we lost all of our eggs when a really big wind tore our nest apart. Another time an eagle swooped in and grabbed one of our chicks. That was a sad day. Other than that, we've been lucky raising at least two chicks every year. Of course, it helps to have two of us," said Oscar.

"I know," said Snowy Pea. "I had a mate. His name was Pepper Pea. He had just finished making our nest when a big hawk appeared from nowhere and grabbed him. It flew away and I never saw Pepper Pea again," she said. "I was so upset, and I didn't know what to do. I was ready to lay my eggs, but I knew it wasn't safe at that beach. So I flew over here hoping this beach would be safer. I've never made a nest before, but I did the best I could and finished this nest just in time. Here are my eggs." Snowy Pea moved away so they all could see her eggs. There were three little sand-colored spotted eggs surrounded by a few small seashells. "I've laid eggs four different times and never hatched one chick. Now that Pepper Pea is gone, I don't have any help to keep them safe," she said sadly.

"That's too bad," said Oscar.

"I have a mate," interrupted Crazy Crow. "Her name is Candy Crow because she always finds candy and sweet things in garbage cans."

"Very interesting, Crazy Crow," said Edna, "but what can we all do to help Snowy Pea?"

Paulie Pelican was the biggest and slowest bird of the group, but he was also very smart. He said, "I have an idea. Let's take turns staying with Snowy Pea until her eggs hatch."

"Great idea," said Oscar. "But, how are we going to do that? I have a family to feed."

"And I have to be with Candy," said Crazy Crow.

Paulie said, "I think I know how we can do it."

THREE

THE SNOWY PEA PROTECTION PLAN

Curious about what Paulie Pelican was planning, the birds stood and stared at him in silence. Paulie stood tall on his big webbed feet and asked, "Snowy Pea, how long will it take your eggs to hatch?"

Snowy Pea thought for a few seconds and said, "I laid my eggs five days ago, so I think they will hatch in about twenty-four days."

"Well, we need to watch the eggs every minute of the day for twenty-four days," said Paulie.

"Wow, that's a long time!" said Oscar.

Then Edna Egret said, "Yes, it's a long time, but it's still a great idea. I suppose Eddy Egret can do without me for a couple of hours a day."

"OK," said Paulie, still figuring. "There are four of us. If we each promise to stand guard for two hours a day, that's eight hours of protection. But, then she will be alone for sixteen hours."

"I know!" said Edna. "We can all go out and get more helpers. I have friends who feed on the beach all day long. I can ask them to assist us."

"Good," said Paulie. "If we each find two helpers, it would give us eight more. So, eight plus the four of us equals twelve guards. That should cover the whole day and night."

"That's an excellent plan! We can call it the Snowy Pea Protection Plan," said Crazy Crow.

"I like that," said Paulie. "The Snowy Pea Protection Plan."

"I can help," said a little voice behind Edna Egret's feet.

They all looked down and saw a small sand-colored crab about the size of a flattened ping pong ball. It had tiny, black, BB eyes perched on top of little stems. It also had two pincers, one much bigger than the other. The little crab had been listening to the birds the whole time.

"Who are you?" asked Oscar.

"I'm Ghosty Ghost Crab," he announced cheerfully.

When Snowy Pea looked at the little ghost crab, she panicked. *Peep! Peep! Peep! Peep!* she cried, as she stood up and flapped her wings.

"Snowy Pea, what's wrong?" asked Paulie Pelican.

"Get him away!" begged Snowy Pea. "A gang of ghost crabs ate my eggs last year! And they attacked my friend's new chicks!"

"Wait! Please!" begged the little crab. "I don't eat bird eggs, or chicks either. I know that other ghost crabs do, but I don't!" he insisted. "That's why I can help watch Snowy Pea's nest."

Yum, another tasty snack, thought Crazy Crow, looking down at the little crab.

"Wait a minute," said Paulie Pelican. "If ghost crabs eat eggs and baby birds, why don't you? You're a ghost crab. What makes you so different?"

"I'm different because I choose to be different," Ghosty said in his tiny voice. "I know what Snowy Pea is going through because one day a big bully ghost crab ate my babies. They had just hatched in the water and were coming onto the beach for the first time. I yelled at him to stop, but he didn't. He just told me that I'd get over it. He was so mean. After that happened I vowed I would never be a cruel ghost crab like he was. Then he got mad and told all the ghost crabs on the beach to ignore me. So I'm on my own and really want to help Snowy Pea."

"You're so little, how could you possibly help?" asked Oscar.

Ghosty Ghost Crab walked up to Snowy Pea and said, "Snowy Pea, please believe me. I won't hurt you. I want to help. I know how important your babies are to you. I have very strong

pincers, and my eyes can see in every direction, day or night. I know all about ghost crabs and I can see them when they're coming to attack your nest."

Snowy Pea sensed that the little ghost crab was telling the truth and relaxed. "Paulie, what do you think?" she asked.

"We could use more help, especially since this little crab can see so well," said Paulie.

"I still don't know how he can help keep big predators away from the eggs," said Oscar. "It seems to me they would eat him, too."

"See this pincer?" said Ghosty, holding up his biggest claw. He snapped it open and shut with amazing force. "I can't reach a raccoon's tail, but I can give it a nasty pinch on its back foot."

Crazy Crow still thought Ghosty looked like a nice snack and wanted to prove he was lying. "I don't believe you, Ghosty Ghost Crab. Go ahead, pinch my leg," Crazy Crow said.

"OK, I will," said Ghosty Ghost Crab as he inched sideways up to Crazy Crow's leg. He clamped onto it with a mighty pinch.

Caw! Caw! Cawwww! shouted Crazy Crow in great pain. He flew several feet straight up into the air with Ghosty still clamped onto his leg.

Ghosty finally let go and fell to the sand. Everyone laughed when Crazy Crow landed on the sand and puffed up his black feathers. "I believe you," he said, looking at his sore leg to see if there was any blood running down it. He decided the little crab might be able to help after all.

"Well, Ghosty Ghost Crab," said Edna Egret, "I think you are very brave. Paulie, do you think he can help?"

"I think we can use all the help we can get," said Paulie Pelican. "Snowy Pea, what do you think? Can you trust this ghost crab?"

Snowy Pea looked at Ghosty and said, "Yes, I suppose I can."

"So that's settled!" announced Paulie. "Now let's go and find new helpers. We will meet back here before the sun sets."

"What about Snowy Pea?" asked Edna. "She'll be alone again if we all leave."

"That's a good point," said Paulie. "I'll stay with Snowy Pea until you come back. Then I'll go and find two more helpers."

Paulie, Snowy Pea, and Ghosty watched as the birds flew off in different directions.

Snowy Pea was curious about the little crab and asked him, "Why are you called a ghost crab?"

"I guess it's because I'm the color of the sand, which makes me almost invisible. It's like I'm a ghost, especially at night when I go out to eat," explained Ghosty. "And I can disappear really fast."

"Oh, that's good," said Snowy Pea. "Then predators won't be able to see you when you go to pinch them."

"That's right," said Ghosty. "Thank you for trusting me, Snowy Pea. You won't regret it. I need to get some rest if I'm going to be on guard. See you later." He disappeared into his deep hole in the sand. Paulie Pelican watched Ghosty leave. He still had an uneasy feeling about the little crab.

"I hope we can trust that crab," said Snowy Pea.

"Don't worry. We'll watch him carefully."

"Thanks, Paulie," said Snowy Pea, hoping the plan would work.

Four

Gathering of the Guards

Edna Egret knew just where to find a couple of guards. She flew down the beach and around the bend where Willie Willet was usually feeding. Edna's wings flapped slowly and gracefully as she reached cruising speed with her long slender neck folded in an S-shape. It wasn't long before she saw Willie pecking at the wet sand with his long sharp bill. He was eating little mole crabs, bugs, and worms.

"Willie!" Edna called as she approached the long-legged brown bird.

"Hi, Edna, how's your day going?" asked Willie Willet, looking up and swallowing a worm.

Edna told Willie about Snowy Pea's struggle to hatch her eggs and explained the Snowy Pea Protection Plan.

"Oh, I remember when my eggs were eaten by a raccoon," said Willie. "I know how it feels. I would be happy to help, but only for two hours a day."

On their flight back to Snowy Pea's nest they saw Iris Ibis scratching in the shallow water with her long, red, curved bill searching for morsels of food. She looked up when Edna and Willie landed in front of her. Edna told her about Snowy Pea and the Protection Plan. Although Iris had never helped little birds before, she thought it was a great idea and said she would do the best she could.

In the meantime, Crazy Crow found Joker Laughing Gull. Joker was standing next to his best friend, Ringer Ring-bill Gull. They were both laughing because Joker had just told a joke. When Crazy Crow reached them, Joker asked if he wanted to hear a joke.

Crazy Crow said, "Tell me later, Joker. Right now I have to tell you guys about the Snowy Pea Protection Plan."

"What's a Snowy Pea?" asked Joker.

"Snowy Pea is a little snowy plover shorebird. Her name is Snowy Pea because she's tiny, like a little pea."

"Oh," said Joker. He thought for a minute, and then asked, "What do you get when you put a laughing gull and snowy plover in a pile of grass?"

"I don't know, what?" asked Crazy Crow.

"A laughing plover in the clover! Ha, ha, ha, hee, hee, hee!" laughed Joker.

"Ha, that's a good one," said Crazy Crow.

Ringer Ring-bill laughed along with Crazy Crow. He was Joker's best friend and always laughed at Joker's jokes, whether they were funny or not.

Crazy Crow told the two gulls all about the Snowy Pea Protection Plan. "What about it?" he asked. "Are you guys willing to help?"

Both Joker and Ringer Ring-bill thought it over for a minute. They decided it might be a lot of fun. They also knew that if something awful happened to Snowy Pea, and her eggs were left alone, they could enjoy a nice snack of bird eggs. So they agreed to help.

"We better go now," said Crazy Crow. The three birds took off toward Snowy Pea's nest.

In the meantime, Oscar Osprey found Ruddy Turnstone and Sandy Sanderling pecking in the wet sand on the other end of the beach. He told them about Snowy Pea's sad story and the Protection Plan. They both said they would gladly help stand guard. Sandy Sanderling really did feel sorry for Snowy Pea, but Ruddy Turnstone was also thinking about the delicious eggs, just in case they were abandoned. Eggs were one of his favorite snacks.

All the birds flew back to Snowy Pea's nest almost at the same time. It was quite a sight. Big birds, little birds, and middle-sized birds, all gathered around tiny Snowy Pea.

Five

Introduction of the Guards

When the birds had settled around the nest, Paulie Pelican said, "Introduce yourselves to Snowy Pea, and I'll go find two more guards." He stretched out his enormous wings, flapped them several times, ran a few steps, and flew up and away.

Willie Willet approached Snowy Pea and said, "I'm Willie Willet, don't worry while I'm around. I can poke any creature with my strong bill and it will never come back again."

"Thank you, Willie," said Snowy Pea.

When Ruddy Turnstone saw Snowy Pea, he thought she looked kind of cute. He liked her right away and decided he didn't want to eat her eggs after all. He walked up to the nest and said, "Hello, Snowy Pea. My name is Ruddy Turnstone. Some call me Rudy, but that's not right. I am called Ruddy because of the color of my feathers. See, they are more reddish than brown." Ruddy spread his wings to show his reddish feathers. "I will do my best to keep your eggs safe. I know what it's like to lose them. Our nest is on the ground, and even though we've hatched many chicks, we've also lost a lot."

Sandy Sanderling quickly scampered up to Snowy Pea. Sanderlings always look like they are sprinting on their little black stick legs. That's how they catch tiny coquinas rolling on the sand as the waves recede back to the ocean. She said, "My name is Sandy Sanderling. I think I'm your cousin because we look so much alike. I lay eggs on the ground and know what you're going through. I'm small, but I'll do what I can to help."

"Thank you," said Snowy Pea.

"Ha, ha, ha, hee, hee, hee," giggled Joker, as he hopped over to Snowy Pea. "I'm Joker Laughing Gull. I tell lots of jokes to make everyone laugh. Want to hear one?" he asked.

"I would love to hear a joke," said Snowy Pea, delighted with all the birds wanting to help her.

Joker walked over to Ringer Ring-bill and asked, "Ringer, did you hear Paulie Pelican give an order to Willie Willet?"

"No, what did he say?" asked Ringer Ring-bill.

"Willie do it!" said Joker.

"I don't know," said Ringer. "Will he do what?" he asked.

Joker and Ringer laughed and laughed. "Get it? Will-he do it." Only Crazy Crow joined Joker and Ringer in the laughter.

"Good grief, Joker," said Edna Egret. "That's a terrible joke."

Snowy Pea didn't know whether to laugh at the joke or Joker laughing at his own joke. So she just chuckled.

Ringer Ring-bill Gull was still laughing when he walked up to Snowy Pea to introduce himself. He said, "I'm Ringer Ring-bill. I'm a gull, and I have a black ring around my bill. That's one way you can tell me apart from Joker and other gulls. My bill is very sharp, so don't worry, I will peck anything that comes close to your eggs while I'm on watch," Ringer reassured her.

"Thank you," said Snowy Pea. "It's my dream to hatch my eggs and see my baby chicks. With your help, maybe my dream will come true." They all agreed.

"Wait, you haven't met this beautiful bird yet," Edna Egret said, looking at Iris Ibis.

Iris Ibis walked slowly up to Snowy Pea and said, "I'm looking forward to helping you hatch your chicks, and I am big enough to scare away any enemies."

"Thank you, Iris," said Snowy Pea, noticing Iris's long, red, curved bill.

Just then Paulie Pelican returned with Blacky-belly Plover and Royal Tern.

"Hello, Snowy Pea, I'm Blacky, a black-bellied plover. I guess you could say we're cousins because we're both plovers, but as you can see, I'm much bigger than you."

Snowy Pea said, "You have very beautiful black feathers on your belly. But since you are much bigger than I, how can you be a cousin?"

"See, my bill is shaped like yours," said Blacky, lifting her bill. "And I have big, round, black eyes like yours. I don't always have this many black feathers on my front, though. It's just when I'm looking for a mate in the springtime that my belly feathers turn black."

Paulie spoke up and said, "Snowy Pea, here is one more helper. This is Royal Tern."

Royal Tern strutted up to Snowy Pea and in a very aristocratic-sounding voice said, "Ms. Pea, I am Royal Tern. It will be my honor to help guard your eggs."

"Thank you, Royal," Snowy Pea said. "Are you a cousin of Joker and Ringer?"

"Heavens no!" Royal replied, standing as tall as he could with his black head feathers extending backward from his head. "I am much more refined and polite than those two gulls."

"Ha!" shouted Joker, feeling insulted. Then he asked, "Did anyone hear the story about the royal tern who was looking for food on the beach?"

"No," replied several birds at once.

"Well, I'll tell you," Joker said.

There once was a tern named Royal,
whose parents surely did spoil.
He demanded some fish
on his favorite dish,
but all he got was fish oil.

"Ha, ha, ha, hee, hee, hee!" Joker laughed and laughed at his own joke. "Ha, ha, ha, hee, hee, hee! Get it? Fish oil? Ha, ha, hee, hee!"

Ringer Ring-bill and Crazy Crow joined in on the laughter. They created quite a noisy commotion.

"Well!" said Royal, feeling very insulted. "That is not even funny, and you all are very rude."

"OK, point made," said Paulie. "But now we have to focus on the reason we're here. Let's make a schedule so Snowy Pea can be safe until her eggs hatch."

"Don't forget me!" said a tiny voice. Ghosty Ghost Crab had emerged from his burrow. Some of the birds, especially the gulls, turned around to see the little crab. They thought he looked like a perfect snack.

Paulie Pelican said, "Everyone, this is Ghosty Ghost Crab. Ghosty is going to help watch the nest at night. He's a part of our team, so don't anyone touch him," he warned. "He can be vicious with his big pincer, and we need his help."

"Do you have any crab friends you could introduce me to?" Ringer asked Ghosty, still thinking of a delicious crab meal.

"No!" said Ghosty, knowing that one day he might be mistaken for another ghost crab.

"Please don't hurt Ghosty," said Snowy Pea. "He can really help us at night, and he does have a powerful pincer."

"That's for sure," said Crazy Crow, whose leg still had pincer marks on it.

"OK, then," said Paulie. "It's time to organize the guards." He assigned each bird to a specific time of day or night. There were some disagreements, but finally everyone agreed to the schedule. The birds had never been a part of a team with a purpose before. All of them were feeling good about protecting Snowy Pea.

Ghosty Ghost Crab felt good, too. Even though he was very little, he had a big assignment—to help with the night watch. He also knew that a lot of the other guards liked to eat crabs, so he decided to be extra cautious while he was standing guard.

Six

Week One—Friends and Foes

The Snowy Pea Protection Plan began right away with Edna Egret standing watch for two hours. Paulie Pelican told Ghosty Ghost Crab to rest because he would be up all night. Then he told the others they could go. "Be sure to remember your two-hour schedule each day for Snowy Pea," he said. They all agreed.

It took a couple of days for the guards to get used to their new schedules, but it was working out very well. Ghosty told Snowy Pea all about ghost crabs and how they eat bird eggs, sea turtle eggs, and newly hatched baby birds when they are weak and unable to defend themselves. Ghosty also told Snowy Pea that he liked her a lot and he liked being a part of the Protection Plan. It made him feel important.

"You are a nice crab, Ghosty, and I appreciate your help," Snowy Pea said. She had gotten over her fear of him. Knowing he was around made her feel safer.

One night Ghosty proved his loyalty by keeping several other ghost crabs away from the nest. He clicked his big pincer and chased them away.

Snowy Pea and Ghosty would often stand together admiring the eggs.

"Gee, Snowy Pea, I almost feel like a dad again," Ghosty told her. "I can't wait until the chicks hatch."

For several days into the first week everyone was happy with the way things were going. But on the fifth day, Snowy Pea had a big scare when Joker Laughing Gull was standing guard. Snowy Pea was sorting through dried seaweed looking for sand fleas when Joker noticed a big dog running down the beach toward the nest. Joker called to Snowy Pea, "Aha, ha, heeee, heeee, heeee! Snowy Pea, come and sit on your eggs. Hurry!" he yelled.

Alarmed, Snowy Pea flew to her nest and nestled down on top of her eggs while Joker flew off toward the big dog. He landed right on the dog's face and poked it on the top of its head with his sharp bill. The poor dog didn't know what had hit him. It stopped short, yelped, and ran back to its owner with its tail between its legs. Joker flew back to Snowy Pea.

"Oh my goodness, Joker. I was so scared that dog was going to run over my eggs," said Snowy Pea. "You are such a brave gull!"

"No problem, Snowy Pea," said Joker, feeling courageous. "That's why I'm here. And to cheer you up, I just thought of a little verse! Would you like to hear it?"

"Sure," said Snowy Pea.

"OK, here it goes," said Joker.

There once was a dog named Dandy,
who loved to run on the sand-y.
He ran down the beach,
Snowy's eggs he'd soon reach,
but his head ran into a Joker!

Joker laughed and laughed. "Ha, ha, ha, hee, hee, hee!"

Snowy Pea giggled. She didn't think the verse rhymed, but she loved when Joker tried to make her laugh. "That was funny, and you have made me feel much better," she told him. Joker decided right then that he would protect Snowy Pea and her eggs with his life.

The rest of the week went smoothly, with most of the birds arriving at the nest on time. The only one who had trouble was Crazy Crow. He missed his watch completely.

"I couldn't help it," Crazy Crow explained to Snowy Pea and Paulie Pelican. "I was searching for food in a garbage bin, when all of a sudden a big wind blew the lid closed. It almost crushed me! See, I have feathers missing on top of my head," Crazy Crow said, trying to get sympathy. "I squawked and squawked for what seemed like a whole day until finally a human lifted the lid to throw in some garbage. Then I flew away and didn't even get to eat anything." He looked at Paulie, who still looked angry. "I'm sorry," Crazy Crow added with his head down. "But look what I found on my way back, Snowy Pea! I brought you a pretty present," he said, thinking it would make her feel better and forgive him.

Snowy Pea and Paulie saw a shiny object with a red ring attached to it next to Crazy Crow's feet. They didn't know what it was, but thought it was nice of Crazy Crow to think of bringing a present.

"Thank you, Crazy Crow," said Snowy Pea. She felt sorry that Crazy Crow went through such a terrible experience. "I'm just glad you're safe," she added.

Paulie was still upset that Crazy Crow missed his watch. He said, "Fortunately for you, Crazy Crow, Snowy Pea is all right because Ruddy Turnstone wouldn't leave the nest until another guard arrived for duty."

"Oh, good," said Crazy Crow. "I will thank Ruddy for staying when I see him again."

Ruddy Turnstone was a good guard. He was bigger than Snowy Pea and had a strong bill that he used to turn over big shells and sticks to find things to eat. One day he brought Snowy Pea a big mole crab. She was delighted that he was so generous. Ruddy was glad to help Snowy Pea, not only because he liked her, but also because he liked being a part of a team with a purpose. He was a tough little bird and very good at chasing away other birds that came near the nest.

It was very quiet at the nest until one morning, Ringtail Raccoon came out from behind a clump of sea oats sniffing for food. He obviously didn't learn his lesson the first time and wasn't aware that Oscar Osprey happened to be on guard at the nest. Snowy Pea was sleeping when Oscar saw the raccoon. He didn't want to wake her up, so he quietly walked away from the nest and went to Ghosty Ghost Crab's hole. He scratched the sand, and Ghosty's eyeballs popped up out of the hole. "What's up?" Ghosty asked.

"Ghosty, go to the nest and stand guard while I take care of that raccoon over there."

"He's not very smart, is he, Oscar?" said Ghosty, remembering the first attack.

"No, he's not. Now go to the nest," Oscar ordered, and took off toward the raccoon. Ringtail Raccoon looked up just in time to see Oscar, with talons spread apart, flying straight toward him. The raccoon suddenly remembered his sore tail and managed to scamper back under the brush just before Oscar reached him.

Ghosty thanked Oscar for scaring away the raccoon. Oscar said, "Don't tell Snowy Pea about the raccoon. She'll just get upset. You keep those ghost crabs away. You're doing a good job," he added.

Ghosty did do a good job keeping other crabs away from the nest. When he couldn't chase them away, he told them the big bird standing watch would eat them if they came anywhere near the nest. One morning at the end of the first week, a big nasty ghost crab ignored Ghosty's warning and went around to the back of the nest to check out the eggs. Unfortunately for him, Ringer Ring-bill was standing guard. Ringer saw the crab approaching and knew it wasn't Ghosty because of its size. He remained still while the sneaky crab moved closer to the nest. With one big jump, Ringer grabbed the ghost crab with his big bill, shook it, and started to eat it.

Snowy Pea awoke to the sound of crunching shells. She saw Ringer tearing apart the ghost crab. "No!" she said in alarm. "Ghosty!"

Just then Edna Egret flew in for guard duty and saw Ringer eating the crab. "Oh, no! You ate Ghosty Ghost Crab. Paulie told you not to do that. How could you?"

Before Ringer could swallow his big mouthful of crab and tell everyone it wasn't Ghosty, Ghosty came out of his hole wondering what all the noise was about.

"What's going on?" he asked, as he scurried sideways to the nest.

Edna saw Ghosty and said, "Ghosty! Thank goodness you're alive! We thought Ringer ate you."

"So did I," said Snowy Pea, relieved to see Ghosty.

"I'm OK," said Ghosty. "Remember I warned you that there would be other ghost crabs feeding on the beach."

Ringer swallowed a piece of crab and said, "Yes, but all ghost crabs look alike except that you're so small. That's how I knew it wasn't you."

"Maybe he should have a signal, so we would know it's really Ghosty," suggested Edna Egret.

"Good idea," said Snowy Pea.

"I know," said Ghosty, "I can click my big pincer three times like this, *Click! Click! Click!* Ghosty showed them again, only louder. *Click! Click! Click!*

"That's great, Ghosty!" said Edna. "Let's make sure all the other guards know about the signal."

They all hoped Ghosty wouldn't need to use his new signal, but that night he did. It was very dark and Joker was hungry. He saw what he thought was another sneaky ghost crab and almost jumped on it. *Click! Click! Click! Click! Click! Click!* signaled Ghosty as Joker approached him with a hungry look in his eyes.

"Oh, it's you, Ghosty. Sorry, I'm just really hungry," said Joker. "I almost forgot about your signal."

"Please don't forget about it again," said Ghosty, relieved that he hadn't been eaten.

"I know how we can remember your signal," said Joker. "Here's a poem."

Click! Click! Click!
I know it's Ghosty Ghost Crab.
Click! Click! Click!
I know he isn't bad.
Click! Click! Click!
Signals Ghosty Ghost Crab,
Click! Click! Click!
Hurt him and I'll be mad!

"I like that," said Ghosty, clicking his big pincer again three times.

When all the birds heard Joker's new poem, they loved it, especially since it did help them to remember the signal.

"Thanks, everyone," said Ghosty. *Click! Click! Click!* "See, my pincer is stronger than ever." It was a good thing his pincer was stronger, because he was going to need it.

SEVEN
Week Two — Disaster at the Nest

On the tenth day of the Protection Plan, Willie Willet was guarding the nest. Ringer Ring-bill walked up to chat with Willie and Snowy Pea. He saw humans having lunch on the beach and remembered Crazy Crow's story of stealing potato chips.

"Snowy Pea, would you help me get some treats like you did with Crazy Crow?" Ringer asked.

Snowy Pea looked down the beach and saw the humans having a picnic. I'd be happy to help you," she said. "Willie, please guard the nest, and if there is any trouble, call us right away."

"Don't worry, I'll stay right here," Willie said. He moved close to the nest and watched his friends.

Snowy Pea flew over to the humans and landed in front of them. She performed her "injured" walk, going around in circles, dragging her wing, and crying, *Peep! Peep! Peep!* The humans stopped eating to watch her. While they watched, Ringer Ring-bill flew in from behind and grabbed something out of a man's hand. Then Snowy Pea and Ringer flew back to the nest.

"That was amazing," said Willie Willet. "Ringer, what did you get?"

Ringer landed with half of a hot dog hanging from his bill. He dropped it in the sand and offered some to Snowy Pea. She thanked him, but she said she was full.

"Have some, Willie," said Ringer.

Willie looked at the meat and said, "Yuck! That looks gross."

"Try it, it's good," said Ringer, pecking out a piece of the meat.

Willie didn't want to be impolite, so he speared a tiny piece and swallowed it. "That's not bad, but I prefer live worms," he said.

Crazy Crow and Joker flew to the nest to see what was going on. They both loved human food and helped Ringer Ring-bill eat the rest of the hot dog. Afterward, they all sat around the nest and talked. Ghosty Ghost Crab joined them, clicking his big pincer, *Click! Click! Click!*

Then Edna Egret arrived for her guard duty.

Snowy Pea told everyone how Joker saved the eggs when a big dog was going to run over them. They were all very impressed with Joker's courage and congratulated him for being such a brave guard.

Joker decided to tell a joke. "What do you call a dog who can fly, is meaner than any dog in the world, and whose name is Oscar?" he asked.

"I don't know," said Snowy Pea.

"Wait a minute," said Ringer. "Oscar is an osprey and dogs don't fly."

"This is a joke, just pretend," said Joker.

"I know!" said Crazy Crow. "Oscar, the meanest flying dog in the world."

"You're close, but that's not it. Give up?" asked Joker.

"Yes!" they all said.

"You call him—Oscar Flyer Meaner Dog!" Joker said, and he laughed and laughed at his own joke. "Get it?" he said. Then he sang a little tune. "I wish I were an Oscar Flyer Meaner Dog."

"Joker, you really have to work on your jokes," said Edna.

"I liked it," said Crazy Crow, singing along.

Then Ringer Ring-bill joined in. "I wish I were an Oscar Flyer Meaner Dog."

Snowy Pea was pleased that her guards were enjoying themselves. She liked having them around the nest because it made her feel safe and not alone.

Since he had an audience, Joker thought he would impress everyone, including Edna, with more of his poetic skills. "Hey, everyone, do you want to hear a poem I just made up about Ringer Ring-bill?"

"Oh boy! Another poem from Joker," said Crazy Crow.

"Great! A poem about me," said Ringer Ring-bill.

"Yes, Joker," said Snowy Pea. "Tell us a poem."

"OK, here it goes," Joker said as he walked in front of the group and cleared his voice.

A guy having lunch
was about to munch
on a hot dog he held in his hand.
He could clearly see
the bird Snowy Pea
dragging her wing in the sand.
He didn't know
if he should go
and help the little bird.
Then Ringer flew by,
grabbed the food from the guy
and left without saying a word.

"That was a wonderful poem and exactly how it happened," said Snowy Pea.

"Actually, Joker, it was a pretty good poem," said Edna Egret, who wanted to encourage Joker to keep practicing his rhymes.

"Thanks," Joker said, happy his poem was a success.

They were all talking about Joker's joke and poem when Royal Tern arrived for his guard duty.

"Hello, Royal," Snowy Pea said politely.

The birds decided to leave because they didn't want to hear Royal brag about himself. They said good-bye to Snowy Pea and flew away until the next watch.

Left by themselves, Snowy Pea told Royal that she was tired and wanted to nap. It was easy for her to feel sleepy with Royal's nonstop chatter. He especially liked to talk about his good looks and how all the girl terns wanted to be with him. Snowy Pea had heard it all before and finally fell asleep.

Suddenly Snowy Pea was startled awake when Harry Herring Gull walked up to the nest. Herring gulls are much bigger than laughing gulls and ring-billed gulls. When Snowy Pea saw the big gull, she became nervous. Harry was not only big, but he looked mean and dishonest.

"My name is Harry Herring Gull and I seem to be lost. Could you tell me where I am?" he asked.

Snowy Pea sensed something was terribly wrong. But before she could say anything, Harry looked at Royal and said, "Oh my, you certainly are a handsome bird."

"Well, thank you," said Royal. He stood tall and puffed up his feathers, feeling flattered.

"Royal, be careful!" Snowy Pea warned. "We don't know this bird!"

"Royal, what a nice name," said Harry. "You are such a good-looking tern, I wonder if you would walk around in a big circle so I can admire your handsome feathers."

"I'd be happy to," said Royal, ignoring Snowy Pea's warning. He couldn't wait to show off his handsome body. He tried to look like a prince as he strutted slowly around in a big circle with his head held high. He walked farther and farther away from the nest. The scheming herring gull suddenly turned toward Snowy Pea. He put his big head down, opened his large bill, and with a mean look in his eyes, chased Snowy Pea away from her nest. He grabbed an egg out of the nest and started to eat it.

Peep! Peep! Peep! screamed Snowy Pea. *Peep! Peep! Peep! Peep! Peep! Peep!*

Royal Tern stopped walking. He looked over at the nest and froze with fear. He saw Snowy Pea away from her nest, flapping her wings and crying out. Then he saw Harry Herring Gull eating one of her eggs.

Ghosty Ghost Crab appeared out of nowhere and saw what was happening. He ran over to Harry and clamped onto his leg with all his might. Harry turned toward Ghosty and was about to grab him when Paulie Pelican flew in and landed right on top of the big gull. Paulie held Harry down with his huge webbed feet while Ghosty kept pinching his leg.

Harry Herring Gull couldn't see what held him helplessly pinned down into the sand. All he could do was scream in pain.

Harry's screams caught the attention of Oscar Osprey, who was soaring over the water looking for fish. Oscar knew something was horribly wrong and flew to the nest as fast as he could.

Paulie was still holding Harry down when Oscar landed. "What's going on?" he asked.

Paulie said, "We have had a terrible tragedy here. I think this cruel, sneaky thief needs to take a trip out to sea."

Oscar looked at Harry with Ghosty clamped onto his leg. Then he looked at Snowy Pea who was staring down at her two remaining eggs. He saw bits of eggshell beside the nest and knew exactly what had happened. He also knew what to do. Paulie stepped off of Harry while Oscar grabbed his back and wings with his big talons. Ghosty let go of Harry's leg.

"You know where to take this nasty creature," Paulie said to Oscar.

"I sure do," said Oscar. With Harry Herring Gull, held securely in his talons, Oscar flew off in the direction of the open gulf. Harry's head was pointing straight ahead as Oscar had adjusted his grip on the gull for less air resistance. They flew farther and farther away until they couldn't be seen anymore.

"Thanks for clamping onto that gull's leg, Ghosty," Paulie said. "It was a brave thing to do and I think he would have gotten another egg if you hadn't distracted him."

They both looked over at the nest. Snowy Pea was settling down on top of her two remaining eggs. She was so sad she could hardly stand it.

"Snowy Pea, what happened?" asked Paulie.

Snowy Pea could barely talk, but managed to compose herself enough to answer.

When Snowy Pea finished explaining what had happened, Paulie walked over to Royal Tern and scolded him for being so vain and self-centered. "Snowy Pea could have lost all her eggs and even her own life!" he shouted.

Royal felt horrible. "I'm sorry. I wouldn't be able to live with myself if something happened to you, Snowy Pea. I promise to do all I can to protect you and your eggs from now on."

"You're finished, Royal!" said Paulie angrily. "We can't trust you to stand guard anymore. You think only about yourself, and you'll have to leave. I will take over your guard duty."

Royal Tern didn't feel very royal anymore. He said, "I know I can't stand guard, Snowy Pea, but I'll be close by watching out for you, anyway. I'm really sorry." With his head down, Royal walked away.

It wasn't long before Oscar Osprey returned to the nest without Harry Herring Gull. He joined Paulie and Ghosty, who were next to Snowy Pea in her nest. They stayed around Snowy Pea for a while, silently mourning the loss of her egg.

After an hour or so, Paulie asked Snowy Pea if she was OK. She nodded. Paulie told her he had to go, but she would be safe with Oscar and Ghosty. He assured her he wouldn't be far away.

"Take care of your little eggs, Snowy Pea," Paulie said, and he flew away.

"Oscar, what did you do with Harry?" Ghosty asked.

"Don't worry, Snowy Pea," Oscar said, "That Herring Gull will not be bothering you again. He's on a little island, and it seems something happened to one of his wings during the journey. He can still eat, but he won't be flying anywhere."

Ghosty told Snowy Pea that he would move his burrow closer to the nest and be with her all the time. He started to dig a new hole just a foot away from the nest.

Snowy Pea was exhausted with sorrow. She was determined that nothing else would happen to her eggs. With Oscar on guard and Ghosty closer than ever, she could finally get some rest. Even with the Protection Plan in place, she was beginning to doubt that her chicks would ever hatch.

EIGHT

WEEK THREE—EGG BALLS

It wasn't long before all the birds heard about Harry Herring Gull. They were all sad for Snowy Pea. They knew she wouldn't leave her eggs, so they brought her food when they came to the nest for guard duty.

The day after Snowy Pea had lost her egg, Crazy Crow brought her what looked like a large white egg. It was big, shiny, and slippery, and he could hardly hold onto it with his bill. He dropped it right next to the nest and said, "I found another egg for you, Snowy Pea!"

Snowy Pea looked at the new egg. She knew it wasn't a snowy plover's egg because it was much bigger. It was perfectly round, white, and had dimples all over it.

"You are so thoughtful to bring this to me, but I don't think its a plover's egg. In fact, I don't believe it's an egg at all," she said.

Ghosty emerged from his little burrow and looked at the new egg. Ghosty had a lot of experience identifying bird and turtle eggs and said, "This almost looks like a sea turtle's egg, but turtle eggs don't have dimples." He tapped the object with his big claw. "It doesn't even sound like an egg."

"What does an egg sound like?" asked Crazy Crow, who was very disappointed his find was not an egg.

"Eggs sound more hollow. This thing sounds solid and very hard," Ghosty said with authority.

Joker, Ringer, Oscar, Paulie, Edna, Willie, Sandy, Blacky, Ruddy, and even Iris Ibis flew in to see how Snowy Pea was doing. They all stared at the strange-looking object Crazy Crow had brought to the nest. No one knew what it was.

Iris Ibis said, "I've seen those things across the river on the smooth green grass where I find lots of bugs and worms to eat."

"I've seen them when I go fishing by the river's edge. Sometimes they are stuck in the mud," said Edna Egret. "Just the other day one splashed in the water right next to me. It scared me to death, and I have no idea where it came from."

"That's where I found this one," said Crazy Crow. "It was at the edge of the river in tall grass. I thought it was an egg."

"One day I watched a human walk up to one on the short grass. He hit it with a long stick," said Iris. "Then I saw another human standing in the tall grass. He yelled out, 'Here's your golf ball!'"

"Golf ball? I've never heard of an egg called a golf ball," said Blacky Belly.

"Well, even if it's not an egg, maybe we could pretend it is," suggested Willie Willet. "We can keep it by Snowy Pea's nest, and if anything comes to eat her eggs, they will get a mouthful of a golf ball instead."

"Great idea!" said Paulie Pelican. "We can call it an egg ball."

"I like that," said Ruddy Turnstone. "An egg ball."

"But, what if a predator comes to the other side of the nest?" asked Blacky.

"That's a good point," said Paulie. "Crazy Crow, do you think you can find more of these?"

"I think so," answered Crazy Crow.

"I can help find some," said Iris Ibis.

"And I'll search for them in the river," added Edna Egret.

"Why do we need more?" asked Snowy Pea, thinking two eggs of her own were enough to worry about.

"If we surround your nest with these egg balls, predators will have a hard time getting to your eggs," said Paulie.

"Yeah, and they'll keep ghost crabs out of the nest," said Ghosty.

"Oh, that makes sense," said Snowy Pea.

"OK," said Paulie. "I'll go with Crazy Crow, Edna, and Iris to help find egg balls. They can put them in my pouch, and we will bring them back all at once."

"You're so smart, Paulie," said Sandy Sanderling.

"Well remember, it was Willie Willet's idea in the first place," said Paulie.

Joker Laughing Gull had remained unusually quiet. With all that had gone on, he was thinking of how he could cheer up Snowy Pea.

It was Ringer Ring-bill who asked, "Joker, are you all right? You haven't said one word or told one joke this whole time."

"Ha, ha, hee, hee, hee. Of course I'm OK," said Joker. "I've been trying to think of a new joke about these egg balls."

"Well," said Crazy Crow. "Did you think of one?" They all looked at Joker with great expectations.

"Not yet, but I'm working on it," Joker said.

Sandy Sanderling said shyly, "I've thought of a poem."

Edna said, "Oh good, Sandy, let's hear it."

"OK," said Sandy, quickly walking over to face Snowy Pea. With a dainty little voice, Sandy recited:

Pretty white egg balls
surrounding Snowy's nest.
Pretty white egg balls
protecting all the rest.
Pretty white egg balls
are the first to go.
Pretty white egg balls
keep away the foes.

"That was a wonderful poem, Sandy!" said Edna Egret.

"I love your poem," said Snowy Pea.

"Thanks," said Sandy, proud of her accomplishment.

Paulie said, "OK, let's go get some more egg balls." Paulie followed Crazy Crow, Edna Egret, and Iris Ibis over the trees and houses to the long stretch of short green grass next to the river.

While the egg-ball hunters were gone, Ghosty Ghost Crab remained on the lookout for predators. He also picked up a few sand fleas around the nest for Snowy Pea to eat.

With everyone caring so much for her, Snowy Pea wanted to feel less worried about her two remaining eggs. She expected they would hatch in a couple of days, but she was still afraid that something awful would happen.

A few hours later, Paulie, Iris, Edna, and Crazy Crow returned to the nest. Paulie plopped down on the sand with his pouch full of white egg balls. Iris Ibis, with her long curved bill, picked egg balls out of Paulie's pouch. She placed them around the nest one at a time.

When all the egg balls were out of his pouch, Paulie shook his head to get the stretched skin back to normal. "Wow! I hope I don't have to do that again," he said. "Those egg balls are heavy."

The nest was quite odd-looking with the egg balls surrounding it, but Snowy Pea felt much more protected having them there.

Ghosty Ghost Crab didn't mind the egg balls, even though he couldn't see over them to watch Snowy Pea's eggs. If they could keep him away from the eggs, they would keep other ghost crabs away as well. At least he hoped they would.

Nine

Getting to Know You

Day twenty-two of the Snowy Pea Protection Plan had passed and the birds were excited that the chicks were going to hatch anytime now. The egg balls kept out a few wandering ghost crabs and a stray ruddy turnstone who didn't know about the plan. They even slowed down a little dog who didn't want to step on the circle of white balls.

The next day, just before her guard duty, Iris Ibis was searching the shoreline for little marine worms. She found one and took it to Snowy Pea.

"How are you doing, Snowy Pea?" she asked, as she put the worm in the nest.

"I'm fine, Iris. Thanks for the snack," Snowy Pea said. While eating the worm, she noticed the length of Iris's red curved bill. "Iris, you're a very pretty bird, with blue eyes and a red bill. I have wondered why your bill is so long and curved," she said.

"I never really thought about it," Iris replied. "I guess it's long because I'm so tall, and it's curved to help me dig up mole crabs and other food buried in the sand. It's not always this red, though. My bill and legs turn bright red when I want to attract a mate."

"Oh, are you trying to attract a mate now?" asked Snowy Pea.

"Not anymore. I met my mate this morning," Iris said happily. "His name is Ike, and we're going to build a nest in the mangrove trees on a little island in the bay. There are lots of other ibis and egrets nesting there. It's called a rookery, where many birds nest at the same time."

"You shouldn't be here if you're building a nest and going to be laying eggs," said Snowy Pea with some concern.

"Don't worry. There's enough time for me to stay on guard," Iris replied. "My mate said he would keep building the nest during the time I'm here. He knows how important you are to me, but when it's time to lay my eggs, I will have to leave my watch. I know it won't be long before your chicks hatch. I really want to see your chicks."

"I would like that," said Snowy Pea. She allowed herself to feel a little excitement at the thought of her new chicks. Then she remembered the dangers that were still around.

"I wish my nest was in a tree," she said. "My eggs would be much safer, and I would have lots of chicks."

"I don't know if our eggs are any safer, Snowy Pea," said Iris. "We have to worry about snakes, raccoons, and other predator birds. That's why it's better for us to have lots of families in the rookery. We warn each other of possible danger."

"It sounds like you have your own Iris Ibis Protection Plan," said Snowy Pea. They both laughed.

"You get some rest," said Iris. It was late in the afternoon and a gentle breeze was cooling the hot sand. Snowy Pea and Iris watched the shorebirds eating their last morsels of the day. There were gulls, terns, black-bellied plovers, ruddy turnstones, sanderlings, and willets, all pecking the sand for bugs, mole crabs, and shellfish.

Paulie and his pelican friends were soaring in a V-formation above the water's surface. They were searching for fish. Iris and Snowy Pea watched as the pelicans turned and dove into the water, making big splashes. Paulie lifted his head with his huge pouch full of water and fish. He emptied the water from his pouch, threw his head back, and tried to swallow the fish he had caught. Joker Laughing Gull flew to the top of Paulie's head and grabbed a small fish that was protruding from Paulie's pouch. Snowy Pea and Iris laughed at the funny scene. Even the terns were diving into the water after stray minnows.

"Wow," said Snowy Pea. "I think diving into the water that hard would hurt Paulie's head."

"That's what I thought, until one day I asked Paulie about it," said Iris. "He told me he might look big and heavy, but he is actually very light because his bones are hollow. He can dive straight into the water with his wings flat against his body and not get hurt."

"That's amazing," said Snowy Pea.

"Oh, look, there's Oscar!" said Iris. "Watch. He's going to dive." Oscar fluttered his wings and dropped toward the water. Just before he reached the water's surface, he extended his wings, stretched out his legs, and grabbed a big sea trout with his talons. He flew back up into the air and shook like a dog to get water off of his wings, while at the same time holding onto the wriggling fish. He managed to get the fish facing forward and flew over to Snowy Pea and Iris. He landed next to them and tore the fish apart with his sharp curved bill, while holding onto it with his talons.

"Want some fish?" he asked.

Without being invited, Joker, Ringer, and Crazy Crow landed next to Oscar's fish. "Can we have some?" asked Crazy Crow.

"OK," said Oscar. "There's enough for everyone, but the next time bring some food with you."

While they all shared the fish, Ghosty Ghost Crab appeared and walked up to the half-eaten fish.

"Here, Ghosty, have some fish," said Oscar, moving out of the way. Ghosty grabbed a little piece of meat with his big pincer and took it over to the nest. He put it on top of an egg ball, and said, "This is for you, Snowy Pea."

Everyone was very impressed with Ghosty's generosity and thoughtfulness.

"Thank you, Ghosty," said Snowy Pea. She really didn't feel like eating fish, but didn't want to hurt Ghosty's feelings, either, so she pecked the piece of fish off the egg ball.

"Here, Ghosty," said Oscar. "Come and get some fish for yourself."

Ghosty grabbed another piece of fish and said, "Thanks." He scampered to his burrow and disappeared with the piece of fish in his big claw.

When only bones were left, Blacky Belly arrived for guard duty. The other birds said goodbye and flew away to roost for the night. As the sun was setting, the clouds turned red, orange, and white.

"Hi, Snowy Pea," said Blacky. "How are you doing?"

"Hi, Blacky. I'm good," said Snowy Pea. "The guards and these egg balls are protecting my eggs so well that I'm feeling very hopeful my chicks will hatch."

"That's great. I'm really happy to be a part of your Protection Plan," said Blacky. "My nest is on the ground, like yours, but not here. I'll be flying way up north where I'll find a mate. That won't be before your chicks hatch," she explained. "And, don't worry, I'm really good at sounding the alarm if anything comes near your nest."

Snowy Pea was glad that Blacky was guarding the nest. But she had an uneasy feeling as darkness spread over the beach.

TEN

GHOSTY, THE HERO

Ghost crabs are basically nocturnal, which means they feed at night. Since so many come out at night, it was always challenging for Ghosty to keep them away from the nest. She was determined not to let anything happen to the eggs.

Blacky could guard only one side of the nest. Ghosty told her that he would guard the other side. Many hours went by quietly without any problems. But then, even with a half-moon shining on the beach, Blacky didn't see the big ghost crab approach the nest between her side and Ghosty's side. Suddenly, she heard a tapping on an egg ball. She whispered, "Ghosty?"

Blacky was waiting to hear Ghosty's, *Click! Click! Click*! signal. When she whispered to Ghosty one more time with no answer, Blacky knew the noise came from an intruder. She sounded the alarm as loud as she could: *Peep! Peep! Peep! Peep! Peep! Peep!*

Blacky's alarm woke up Snowy Pea and before she knew what was happening, Ghosty ran around the nest and saw the invading ghost crab. Ghosty raised his big pincer and ran toward the crab with a *Click! Click! Click! Click! Click! Click!*

Even though the crab was bigger than Ghosty, he was afraid of Ghosty's fierce attack and decided to run away. Ghost crabs can run up to ten miles an hour. When the big ghost crab dashed away from the nest, Ghosty chased him down the beach.

"Wow! That was close," said Blacky.

"Thanks for sounding the alarm," said Snowy Pea. "Ghosty is so brave, too."

"Yes, for a little crab, he does have a lot of courage," agreed Blacky, still feeling very nervous.

Snowy Pea settled down on her eggs while waiting for Ghosty to return. Blacky walked around the nest trying to protect all sides. After awhile she became tired and stopped to rest.

"I wish Ghosty would come back," she said, trying to catch her breath.

"Me, too," said Snowy Pea.

They listened for Ghosty. He had been gone a long time. The eastern sky was beginning to lighten with dawn. It was very quiet except for a rustling in the sea grass by the dunes. They thought it might be a mouse running around. But it wasn't long before the noise was closer to the nest. Blacky called out, "Ghosty, is that you?"

When they didn't hear Ghosty's familiar *Click! Click! Click!,* Snowy Pea shook with fear and almost flattened herself down over her eggs to protect them. Blacky slowly walked around the nest. She was startled when she saw a long black snake grab an egg ball and slither away with it.

Both birds sounded the alarm. *Peep! Peep! Peep! Peep!*

Snowy Pea wouldn't leave her eggs. Blacky ran around the nest over and over again, peeping as loud as she could.

Ghosty was not far from the nest when he heard the calls for help. He ran to the nest at top speed. When he got there, he saw that Blacky was in a panic and could barely breathe. Snowy Pea managed to tell Ghosty about a long black snake that took an egg ball. They all looked down the beach. The rising sun was lighting the sky just enough so that Ghosty could clearly recognize the snake moving away with what looked like a huge head.

"That's Sneaky Slicker Snake!" Ghosty said. He sprinted away down the beach toward the snake.

Snowy Pea yelled out, "Ghosty, don't go! That snake will eat you!"

Ghosty knew some snakes will eat ghost crabs, but he ran after it, anyway. When he finally caught up with it, he raised his big pincer and clamped onto the snake's tail with all his might. Sneaky Slicker Snake turned in pain to bite Ghosty, but couldn't because his mouth was full of an egg ball. With the egg ball stuck in his mouth, the snake turned and slithered away in pain into the sea oats. Ghosty had let go of the snake's tail and scurried back to Snowy Pea. Just as he reached the nest, he saw Paulie Pelican next to Snowy Pea.

"Snowy Pea, are you all right?" Ghosty asked.

"I'm fine and so are my eggs, thanks to you and the egg balls," she said.

"Ghosty, you are so brave," said Blacky. "I would never go after a big snake like that. I was scared to death!"

"It was nothing," said Ghosty, pretending he wasn't afraid. "I was just doing my job."

"Well, Ghosty, I must say that at first I didn't trust you. But now, if there was an award for the bravest guard in the Snowy Pea Protection Plan, I would give it to you," said Paulie.

"Blacky, you must be exhausted. Go get some rest," said Paulie. "I'll watch the nest until Oscar comes to stand guard."

"OK," said Blacky, gratefully. She flew down the beach to her favorite roost.

"You get some rest, too, Snowy Pea," said Paulie. "Ghosty and I will make sure you are safe for the rest of the day."

"I'll try," said Snowy Pea.

"I have to go into the water to get some air." Ghosty said. Once in awhile ghost crabs need oxygen from the water to go through their gills. Ghosty needed a lot of oxygen after his heroic activities.

"Be careful," warned Paulie.

"I will," he replied. Ghosty looked around as he walked into the gently breaking waves. He knew about the black-crowned night-heron that walks the shoreline at night to feed. But, since it was early morning, he didn't think the heron would be around.

Eleven

Breakfast with the Guards

Ghosty took in all the oxygen he needed and rode a wave onto the sand. He scurried out of the water, looking in every direction with his BB eyes. Then he spotted the black-crowned night heron wading in the shallow water. It was still fishing for minnows and heading in Ghosty's direction. Ghosty didn't want to take any chances so he quickly dug a hole in the sand to hide. His little eyeballs peeked out of the hole so he could watch the big bird. The heron put his head down and chased a fish just past Ghosty. He caught and swallowed the fish, then looked around for more.

Just as a wave receded, he saw the hole where Ghosty was hiding. Ghosty dug deeper. He was sure his life was about to end. Water and sand flowed into the hole. The heron strode up to Ghosty's hiding place. All of a sudden Paulie Pelican landed right next to the night heron and knocked it over. The heron was so scared, it flew away down the beach. Ghosty popped out of the water-filled hole.

Click! Click! Click! "Wow, Paulie, thanks! I thought I was going to be that heron's breakfast," said Ghosty.

"I was watching out for you, Ghosty," said Paulie. "Now let's go protect Snowy Pea." They walked back to the nest together.

Except for the rhythmic sound of small waves gently rolling onto the sand, silence surrounded the nest again. Even though the sun was rising above the horizon, Snowy Pea finally fell asleep. Paulie stood at the side of the nest where the missing egg ball had left a hole. Ghosty Ghost Crab tried to stay alert on the other side of the nest. He was tired after all his battles, but managed to stay awake for Snowy Pea.

Snowy Pea awoke to the shrill cry of Oscar Osprey soaring over the water. *Cheep! Cheep! Cheep! Cheep!* He had caught a fish and was calling to Snowy Pea to announce that breakfast was coming.

Snowy Pea stretched her legs, then her wings one at a time. She looked at her precious eggs with such affection, that she could hardly stand it. She knew they would be hatching soon.

Oscar landed in front of the nest with the fish still in his talons.

"Ah. I see you have brought breakfast," said Paulie.

"It's for all of us," said the osprey.

From a short distance away, Joker Laughing Gull saw Oscar with the fish. Ringer was with him, and they didn't want to miss a good meal. Upon arriving at the nest, Joker said, "It looks like the night went well and breakfast is ready."

Just then Blacky arrived. "How are you, Snowy Pea?" she asked with concern. "I have been so worried about you."

Before Snowy Pea could answer, Crazy Crow landed in front of the nest with a huge piece of doughnut in his bill. "I brought something for breakfast!" he mumbled, and dropped the treat in the sand.

Then, Willie Willet, Edna Egret, Ruddy Turnstone, Iris Ibis, and Sandy Sanderling arrived and formed a circle around the nest, eager to see if the eggs had hatched yet.

"Good morning. I'm happy to tell you that my eggs are fine, even though we've had a very scary night," Snowy Pea announced.

"What happened?" asked Willie.

Edna Egret noticed an egg ball was missing and said, "Oh no, where is the egg ball?"

Snowy Pea proceeded to tell the group what had happened in the night.

"My goodness!" said Edna.

"Good job, everyone!" said Oscar.

"It looks like the Snowy Pea Protection Plan really works," said Iris Ibis.

"That's right," said Paulie. "From now on we have to be extra watchful that no predator comes near the nest. But for now, let's enjoy the fish and the doughnut." Then he added, "Crazy Crow, after you eat would you please go and find another egg ball to replace the one that snake stole?"

"Sure thing," replied the fish crow. He finished swallowing a chunk of fish, had a bite of doughnut, and flew away toward the river.

"Joker, you haven't told us any jokes," said Ringer.

"I didn't want to take anything away from Ghosty and Blacky, but I was thinking about that snake," said Joker.

"What were you thinking?" asked Ruddy.

"Oh, just that the slippery, slithering, sly, silent, slimy, Sneaky Slicker Snake stole sweet, shy Snowy Pea's egg ball," said Joker, waiting for a reaction.

"Ha, ha, ha, Joker, that's a good one," said Ringer. "Go ahead say that again, only faster."

All the birds had fun taking turns trying to recite Joker's silly snake sentence, and no one could say it without getting mixed up.

Soon Crazy Crow returned to the nest with a replacement egg ball. He put it in place, and Joker announced, "I have a little poem about the snake and the egg ball."

"Joker, you just told us about Sneaky Slicker Snake and the egg ball," said Edna Egret.

"I want to hear another poem," said Ringer.

"OK, here goes," said Joker.

Slicker Snake was looking for cake,
but an egg ball he did take.
He slithered away to hide in the hay,
and he found the egg was a fake.

"Ha, ha, ha, that's a funny one," said Crazy Crow.

"It was pretty good, but you better keep practicing," said Edna Egret.

"Hey, look over there," interrupted Iris, looking down the beach to where a large flock of terns had gathered.

"Oh my," said Edna Egret.

Twelve

Forgiveness and Joy

A little way down the beach, Royal Tern and a large flock of his relatives had landed to eat and rest. Instead of eating, Royal moved away from the flock and stared up the beach toward Snowy Pea's nest.

Oscar, with his excellent eyesight, recognized Royal looking at them. "Guess who's there!" he said.

Paulie looked down the beach and saw Royal Tern staring back at him. Paulie knew he was right in telling Royal to leave his guard duty, but he felt sorry for him as well. He wasn't really a bad bird. He just made a bad choice. Paulie asked, "Snowy Pea, is it OK with you if we invite Royal to come back? Maybe he's learned a lesson."

Snowy Pea looked down the beach at Royal. She had mixed feelings about him. She knew he didn't intentionally cause the loss of her egg. She also knew he was sorry. It was with her big heart and willingness to forgive that Snowy Pea said, "OK."

"Ruddy, go and tell Royal that Snowy Pea has invited him back to the nest," Paulie said.

Ruddy Turnstone was happy to help and flew down the beach to get Royal. When Ruddy told Royal about the invitation, the tern felt happier than he had ever felt in his life. They flew back together.

"Hello, Snowy Pea," Royal said shyly. "I'm happy to see that you and your eggs are safe. I'm sorry about what happened to your egg, and I want to tell you that I've learned a big lesson."

"What did you learn, Royal?" asked Paulie Pelican, who was still angry with him.

"I learned that being conceited and self-centered hurt both Snowy Pea and me. I learned that it doesn't matter what you look like, what matters is what you do. My wise grandmother, Queenie Tern, told me, 'Being a good-looking tern doesn't mean you're automatically a good tern.' She also said, 'If you're a good tern, you do good things.' I've tried to do good things ever since Paulie ordered me to leave the Protection Plan. Now my family is amazed at how kind and considerate I've become."

"That's wonderful," said Snowy Pea. "I am glad you learned a lesson. I forgive you and hope everyone else can as well."

"I guess one good tern deserves another," said Paulie.

"Paulie, are you making a joke?" asked Joker.

"Ha, I think it was," said Paulie. "Now Royal, if you have really learned a lesson, I suppose I can forgive you. What about everyone else?" he asked.

The birds talked it over and finally agreed. Royal had learned a very big lesson about responsibility and loyalty. The other birds learned a lot about forgiveness.

"I know we all make mistakes, and like Royal, we can choose to learn from them," said Edna Egret.

Royal felt proud again, only this time he was proud of the good things he did, not how handsome he looked.

"Thank you, everyone. Now I know what real friendship is," said Royal.

Joker walked over to him. "Royal, I have a poem for you," he announced.

"Oh no!" said Edna Egret.

Royal feared what Joker might say next.

"Wait a minute," said Joker. "I think you all will like this poem." Then he said,

There once was a tern named Royal,
whose mother and father did spoil.
But, a lesson he learned,
and his ways he did turn,
to be kind and good and loyal.

"That's a nice poem," said Edna Egret.

"I like your poem. Thanks," said Royal.

The birds were discussing the poem and how Royal had changed when all of a sudden, Snowy Pea flew straight up into the air and cried, *Peep! Peep! Peep*!" She was so loud it scared all the birds.

As Snowy Pea came back down beside the nest, Paulie asked, "What's wrong?"

"Oh, look!" said Snowy Pea. "An egg is cracking!"

"Oh, my goodness! I think your chicks are hatching!" said Iris Ibis with great excitement.

The birds gathered around the nest to watch.

"Look! That egg is moving!" said Crazy Crow.

Click! Click! Click! "I want to see, too!" *Click! Click! Click!* "I want to see," said Ghosty, who was pounding on an egg ball, trying to get over it. "I can't see the eggs!" he cried. "The egg balls are in my way!"

Iris reached down with her long bill and moved several egg balls out of the way so Ghosty could see the chicks hatching. He was very excited.

Snowy Pea watched her eggs with such joy, she was about to cry. She saw one egg crack and a speck of a black bill stuck out of a little hole in the shell. All the birds watched with happy anticipation.

Crack! The eggshell broke open. A tiny, wet, baby chick emerged. It looked like a big cotton ball with stick legs.

"Oh, how wonderful!" Snowy Pea exclaimed.

"Yippee!" cried Ghosty Ghost Crab, clicking his pincers, *Click! Click! Click!*

Then the other eggshell started to crack. Another tiny black bill emerged. More cracks appeared as the egg rolled back and forth. Out popped a chick's head. The chick fought and fought until the entire shell had broken away.

The birds of the Snowy Pea Protection Plan stood around the nest speechless and joyful. There were two tiny, wet snowy plover chicks in the nest trying to stand and balance on weak, spindly legs.

"My goodness! They are adorable!" said Edna Egret.

"Congratulations, Snowy Pea!" said Willie Willet.

"Hurrahhhhhh!" said Crazy Crow, Joker, and Ringer Ring-bill at the same time.

"They are beautiful!" said Royal Tern.

"They're so cute!" said Sandy Sanderling.

Iris Ibis stared at the chicks with feelings of joy in her heart.

Joker stood watching them, speechless for the first time in his life. He thought he was going to cry with happiness.

"Congratulations to everyone," said Paulie Pelican. "The Snowy Pea Protection Plan is a great success!"

"I can't believe it," said Snowy Pea. "My eggs have hatched. I have two baby chicks at last. Thank you all so much. I am the happiest snowy plover in the world!"

The chicks were still trying to stand on their long, unsteady legs, falling to one side, getting up, and falling over again. They began to dry out, and their tiny feathers puffed up like fuzz.

"Snowy Pea, what are you going to name them?" asked Iris.

Crazy Crow said, "They both look like fuzzy puffballs. You can name one Puffy and the other Fuzzy."

"Wait, I have another idea," said Joker. "They are fuzzy and tiny. You can name one Fuzzy and the other one Pee Wee. Fuzzy Pea and Pee Wee Pea! Ha, ha, ha, hee, hee, hee!"

All the birds laughed at the silly names.

"Snowy Pea should name them," suggested Edna Egret. "She's their mother."

"Snowy Pea, have you thought of any names?" asked Oscar.

"Well, one is a girl and the other is a boy. I want to name the boy Pepper Pea, after his father," she said.

"Yeah, Pepper Pea! That's a great name!" said Ringer.

"You could name the little girl, Snowy Pea, after you," suggested Sandy Sanderling.

"Oh, but she looks so sweet," said Snowy Pea. "I will name her Sweet Pea."

"Pepper Pea and Sweet Pea," repeated Edna Egret. "We are so happy for you, Snowy Pea."

Ghosty Ghost Crab and the birds of the Snowy Pea Protection Plan stayed around the nest admiring the new chicks for most of the morning. The chicks were able to stand and eat by themselves within a few hours. They just needed to strengthen their little legs so they could go from walking to running. Learning to run was most important, especially for running away from predators.

"We need a poem for the chicks," said Joker.

"Good idea," said Edna. "Why don't we go around in a circle, and everyone can add a new stanza?"

"What's a stanza?" asked Crazy Crow.

"A stanza is a certain number of lines in a poem," said Edna Egret, who knew about making up poems.

"I like that idea," said Paulie Pelican. "Edna, since you know how to make up poems, would you mind starting one?"

"Well, thank you, Paulie, I'd be glad to start a poem about the chicks," said Edna. She thought for a minute and then she said,

One day on the beach,
Snowy Pea thought she'd teach
her chicks named Pepper and Sweet . . .

"My turn," said Joker. He continued the poem,

how to play a new game
called Do it the Same,
to win and to get a new treat.

"My turn," said Crazy Crow who loved to play games.

Now here's how to play,
just do what I say,
and follow me through the sea grass.

"I think I can finish," said Snowy Pea.

I will find a sand flea
so the chicks can see
how to catch one because they're so fast.

"Great poem!" said Ringer Ring-bill.

The birds agreed and rehearsed the poem while watching the chicks run about, catching bits of food.

Paulie Pelican interrupted the happy moment and said, "Attention everyone! Our job is not finished yet. Pepper Pea and Sweet Pea are still in danger from predators, especially now, when they can't defend themselves very well. I'm going to stay with Snowy Pea and the chicks until they can fly."

"Good point," said Edna Egret. "Snowy Pea, how long will it take the chicks to learn to fly?"

"Oh, they should be able to fly in about thirty days," said Snowy Pea. "You see, usually I would leave in a week or so to find another mate. Pepper Pea would stay with the chicks until they can fly. But since he's not here, I will stay with them. I wouldn't think of leaving them now," she added.

"You mean if Pepper Pea were alive, you would still go and find another mate?" asked Oscar, not believing what he was hearing.

"Yes," Snowy Pea answered. "That's the way snowy plovers behave."

"Oh, I didn't know that about plovers," Oscar said. "Olive is my mate for life."

Edna Egret said. "What's important now is that Sweet Pea and Pepper Pea survive. I'll be around to keep an eye on them until they can be on their own."

"I'll stay," said Crazy Crow. "Candy can come with me once in a while."

Paulie Pelican looked at all the birds and asked, "I know it's time for some of you to fly north to start your own families, but who else is able to stay here until the chicks can fly?"

Joker Laughing Gull said, "Count me in."

"I'll stay, but only until the chicks can leave the nest," said Ringer Ring-bill. "Then I have to fly north also."

Iris Ibis, Oscar, Royal, and Ghosty Ghost Crab said they could stay the whole time.

"I'll stay as long as I can," said Willie Willet.

Those who had to migrate north right away were Ruddy Turnstone, Sandy Sanderling, and Blacky-belly Plover.

"Well, I think we'll have enough guards to watch the chicks," said Paulie.

Snowy Pea thanked them. "I hope when you come back, you'll bring your families with you," she added.

Everyone gathered together and said their good-byes to the birds who were flying north.

"See you in the fall," called Blacky as they took off together.

"It's sad to see them go," said Willie.

"I know, but they will be back after summer," said Paulie. "Now it's time to get organized for our chick watch," Paulie added.

With the chicks running about, keeping track of them was going to be challenging. But it was good that they were staying, because danger was never far away.

THIRTEEN

A HERO'S REWARD

In a few hours, Sweet Pea and Pepper Pea were having a great time running around the nesting area. They would move farther away as their long legs got stronger. Snowy Pea watched over her new chicks with joy and pride.

The next day was sunny and cloudless. The sun warmed the sand while Sweet Pea and Pepper Pea darted about the beach chasing little sand fleas and bugs. Suddenly, Snowy Pea sounded the alarm. *Peep! Peep! Peep! Peep! Peep! Peep!* she called as she ran around in circles with her wing dragging in the sand.

Ghosty Ghost Crab came up out of his burrow to see what was happening. At the same time Oscar Osprey and Paulie Pelican flew in to see what was going on.

"What's wrong?" asked Ghosty.

When Oscar and Paulie landed next to Snowy Pea, Paulie asked, "What's the matter?"

"Look! They're running after Sweet Pea and Pepper Pea," she cried.

Her friends looked over toward the running chicks and saw a little boy and girl chasing them.

"What can we do?" asked Snowy Pea in a panic.

Paulie whispered something to Oscar and then to Ghosty. Then he said, "Don't worry, Snowy Pea, we will take care of those kids." The two big birds took off.

"Try to be calm, we'll take care of this," said Ghosty as he scampered as fast as he could toward the chicks. She watched helplessly as Paulie flew over the water and dove in bill-first. When he came up his pouch was full with about two gallons of water. He emptied some of it out and with great effort he became airborne with his pouch still full. He headed straight toward the children. At the same time Oscar was approaching the little boy and girl.

Snowy Pea watched Paulie as he flew above the boy and girl. He tipped his bill downward, and dumped water all over them. At the same time, Oscar flew in and tapped the top of their heads with his talons, which caused them to fall to the sand. Then Ghosty scampered over to the little boy and pinched his big toe. Then he pinched the little girl's big toe.

The children were screaming, "Mommy!" They got up and ran as fast as they could down the beach toward their mother. They really didn't know what had happened to them, but they never chased little birds again.

Oscar, Paulie, and Ghosty went back to Snowy Pea, who had gathered the chicks together.

"Thanks for scaring those kids away," said Snowy Pea.

"I'm just glad we were nearby," said Paulie.

"I'm glad you were here," said Ghosty. "I don't think I could have pinched those kids without you knocking them down."

"That was very brave of you, Ghosty," said Snowy Pea.

Joker, Edna, Willie, and Crazy Crow arrived to check up on the chicks. Snowy Pea told them how Paulie, Oscar, and Ghosty had rescued the chicks from the children.

After congratulating them, Snowy Pea said, "Ghosty, you are the smallest and bravest guard in the group. We have all decided that you deserve a medal. Crazy Crow, do you have something for Ghosty?"

"Yes, I do," said Crazy Crow, who picked up a shiny object and held it in his bill. It was a very thin strand of a gold bracelet that Crazy Crow had found in the sand. It had a shiny small #1 hanging from it. Crazy Crow had managed to break the links just to a size that would fit over Ghosty's eye stalks. He took it over to Ghosty and carefully placed it over his BB eyes and head. The gold #1 hung down and almost touched the sand because Ghosty was so short. The birds cheered, "Yea, Ghosty Ghost Crab!"

Ghosty was extremely happy with his new medal, but all he could say was, "Thanks, I'll never take it off."

Ghosty was able to swing his medal around to his back whenever he had to walk or run about. He could still *Click! Click! Click!* his big pincer and chase other ghost crabs away.

Aside from the scare with the children, time passed quickly and safely as Sweet Pea and Pepper Pea grew new feathers. The Protection Plan was still working and allowed them to run freely around on the beach, eat bugs, and flap their little wings every day. Then one day, Pepper Pea discovered he was able to fly a short distance. Soon after, Sweet Pea learned that she could fly. With practice they were both flying longer distances up and down the beach.

Many of the bird friends joined the chicks as they flew all about until the time had come to say good-bye. They all gathered on the beach and formed a circle around the three snowy plovers. Ghosty Ghost Crab walked sideways between Edna Egret's legs into the center of the circle next to Snowy Pea. His medal was hanging from his neck. The chicks were ready to fly away and begin life on their own.

They stood in silence until Snowy Pea said, "Because of your dedication and friendship, my dream has come true. I hope your dreams also come true."

"I think we all should return to this spot next spring and have a reunion," said Paulie.

"Great idea!" said Edna.

Joker said, "I'll have lots more poems and jokes by then."

"I can't wait," said Ringer Ring-bill.

"I'm going to learn how to tell jokes, too, so I can make everyone laugh," added Crazy Crow.

"Just you being you, Crazy Crow, makes us laugh," said Paulie.

The chicks were getting impatient, and Snowy Pea said, "I guess we better think about going. Sweet Pea and Pepper Pea are ready for their new journeys."

The birds said good-bye to each other, then flew off in different directions. Snowy Pea and the chicks said farewell to Ghosty. They promised to return the next spring.

Ghosty watched with a feeling of sadness as the three snowy plovers flew off together. He was left alone on the beach with his little BB eyes looking all around. He glanced at his medal and knew he would see his good friends again. He also hoped he could be a guard in another Protection Plan. He walked sideways to his burrow, stopped at the edge, went *Click! Click! Click!*, and disappeared into the hole in the sand.

ABOUT THE AUTHOR
Kyle L. Miller

Former teacher and tennis coach, author, publisher, wildlife educator, and resident of Sanibel Island, Florida, Kyle Miller weaves environmental and educational lessons into her memorable children's fiction. *Snowy Pea and the Ghost Crab*, introduces youngsters to beach wildlife, and the importance of protecting it. She's also the author of *DILLO - A Baby Armadillo's Adventure on Sanibel Island* (2009 Eric Hoffer Legacy Award in Fiction, First Runner-up).

She was nominated for the 2007 Angel of the Arts Award, for Literary Artist of the Year, presented by The Alliance for the Arts of Lee County, Florida.

To contact Ms. Miller for author presentations, school visits, or publisher presentations, call (239)472-0599, or e-mail: KMiller765@aol.com

ABOUT THE ILLUSTRATOR
Randon T. Eddy

Former teacher and business woman, Randon T. Eddy, is a prolific artist and member of several art leagues in southwest Florida. In 2004 and 2009, Ms. Eddy had a three month one person wildlife art show at the J. N. "Ding" Darling National Wildlife Refuge.

In 2005 Ms. Eddy first ventured into illustrating children's books with, *DILLO – A Baby Armadillo's Adventure on Sanibel Island*, by Kyle L. Miller, which was followed by *DILLO – the Coloring Book*. In 2007 she wrote and illustrated, *The Mysterious Creature*, an early reader picture book, published by Jungle House Publications. Ms. Eddy can be reached by calling: (239) 395-4518.